Walking with You
THROUGH EVERY SEASON

Walking with You

THROUGH EVERY SEASON

Proverbs 31 Through the Eyes of a Coach's Wife

TALISHA ALLIGOOD

Walking with You Through Every Season © Copyright 2023 Talisha Allgood

All rights reserved. No part of this publication may be reproduced, distributed, or transmitted in any form or by any means, including photocopying, recording, or other electronic or mechanical methods, without the prior written permission of the publisher, except in the case of brief quotations embodied in critical reviews and certain other noncommercial uses permitted by copyright law.

Unless otherwise indicated, Scripture quotations taken from the New American Standard Bible®, Copyright © 1960, 1962, 1963, 1968, 1971, 1972, 1973, 1975, 1977, 1995 by The Lockman Foundation. Used by permission.

Scripture quotations marked (ESV) are taken from The Holy bible, English Standard Version®(ESV®), copyright © 2001 by Crossway, a publishing ministry of Good News Publishers. Used by permission. All rights reserved.

Scripture quotations marked (NIV) are taken from the Holy Bible, New International Version®, NIV®. Copyright © 1973, 1978, 1984, 2011 by Biblica, Inc™. Used by permission of Zondervan. All rights reserved worldwide. www.zondervan.com The "NIV" and "New International Version" are trademarks registered in the United States Patent and Trademark office by Biblica, Inc™.

Cover Design and Formatting by Susi Clark of Creative Blueprint Design

TABLE OF CONTENTS

INTRODUCTION		1
PROVERBS 31	ADAPTATION OF PROVERBS 31:10-31	4
PROVERBS 31:10	NO STANDS	7
PROVERBS 31:11	WHO'S GOT YOUR BACK?	11
PROVERBS 31:12	STATUE OF LIBERTY	17
PROVERBS 31:13	ROLL UP YOUR SLEEVES.	21
PROVERBS 31:14	DO YOU NEED APPLIANCES?	25
PROVERBS 31:15	WHAT SLEEP?	29
PROVERBS 31:16	BLOOM WHERE YOU ARE PLANTED	33
PROVERBS 31:17	STRONG ARMS	37
PROVERBS 31:18	SLEEP/REST	41
PROVERBS 31: 19	WORKER BEE	45
PROVERBS 31: 20	WHERE ARE YOU CALLED TO SERVE?	49
PROVERBS 31:21	NO RED	53
PROVERBS 31:22	LOOK GOOD, FEEL GOOD, PLAY GOOD	57
PROVERBS 31:23	DO YOU IRON?	61
PROVERBS 31:24	JEHOVAH-JIREH	65
PROVERBS 31:25	CIRCLE UP	69
PROVERBS 31: 26	CAROLYN CURRY KIND OF KIND	73
PROVERBS 31: 27	CHEESE SANDWICH	77
PROVERBS 31: 28	HAND ON YOUR HEART AND DUMB PLAYS	81
PROVERBS 31: 29	ROLE MODELS	85
PROVERBS 31: 30	PRETTY IS AS PRETTY DOES	91
PROVERBS 31: 31	YOU ARE WELCOME	95
ACKNOWLEDGEMENTS		99
ABOUT THE AUTHOR		103

INTRODUCTION

Thank you for picking up this book. I believe God has a divine plan and purpose in this for you.

I have been a coach's wife for twenty-five years. A lot of changes have taken place over the years, but the one constant is that I always need encouragement and assurance of this calling. This life that God has called us to has many seasons of joy and many seasons of sorrow. It's the never knowing which season it's going to be that gets me. To cope with all the highs and the lows, I must stay saturated in God's Word.

Many years ago, I began jotting down notes and prayers relating to this coaching life. Over the last five years, God has prompted me to focus on Proverbs 31 and write a devotional book from the perspective of a coach's wife.

There are many adjectives that describe the Proverbs 31 woman I feel also describe the coach's wife. She is a hard worker, is resourceful, and takes initiative. She is intelligent, has a lot of energy, and manages her time and resources well. Most of all, she fears the Lord above all else. The fear of the Lord is what allows her to be all the other things this passage describes. She realizes "her worth is far above jewels" and God has created her to walk beside her husband and be his greatest encourager.

I have included several stories and antidotes from some of my mentors and coaching-wife greats who I consider to be shining examples of the Proverbs 31 woman. This has been a long process with a lot of ups and downs and help from some amazing people.

I pray that for those of you who know Jesus Christ as your personal Lord and Savior that God uses this devotional to encourage you and help you to continue to press on and finish the race for which you have been called. Maybe some of you will read these thoughts and not really understand what much of it means. Perhaps God has put this book into your hands to draw you to Himself. If you do not yet know Jesus Christ as your personal Lord and Savior, I pray this devotional will point you to the cross and show you your need for His unconditional love and sacrifice. He loved you so much that He gave His only son for you. Jesus came to die on the cross and take on your sin. Romans 5:8 says, "But God demonstrated His own love toward us, in that while we were still sinners, Christ died for us." If this is you, I hope you will seek Him today. He loves you. He wants to take on your burdens and give you a peace that passes all understanding.

As I have walked through this coaching-wife life, I have gained encouragement from Scripture, and from other wives. Romans 8:28 has been the verse I cling to in all situations. "We know that God causes all things to work together for good for those who love God, to those who are called according to His purpose." Even in those times where this life does not make sense, I have the assurance that He has a plan, and it is greater than anything I can ever imagine.

INTRODUCTION

Every time I have faced challenges or had to move jobs, God has had something bigger and better in store that I never dreamed of. I am learning as Paul says in Philippians 3 to "[forget] what lies behind and [reach] forward to what lies ahead." When the clock runs out and the game of life is over, you want to have the confidence that you have finished well.

PROVERBS 31

Proverbs 31 from a coach's wife's perspective

10 An excellent wife who can find her?
   For her worth is far above touchdowns.

11 The heart of her husband trusts in her,
   And he will have no loss of yardage.

12 She cheers from the stands
   All the days of her life.

13 She looks for a home in a new place,
   And packs boxes into the night.

14 She is like merchant ships;
   She brings her family from afar.

15 And she rises while it is still night
   Heats up leftovers and waits for film work to be completed.

16 She considers the field and helps to paint it;
   From her earnings she buys the string.

17 She surrounds herself with strength
   And makes her arms strong.

18 She senses that her profit is good;
   Only five more yards to a first down.

19 She stretches out her hand when a flag is thrown,
   And her instinct is to question the call.

20 She extends her hands to the boosters,
   And she stretches out her hands to the fans.

PROVERBS 31

21 She is not afraid of a loss,

   For she has walked through that fire before.

22 She orders coverings for herself from the current year's coaching catalog;

   Her clothing is a fine hoodie and sweats in team colors.

23 Her husband is known on all fields,

   When he calls plays like no other.

24 She makes colorful pom poms and sells them,

   And supplies cowbells to all of the fans.

25 Strength and dignity are her clothing,

   And she smiles at the off season.

26 She opens her mouth in chants,

   And the teaching of cheers is on her tongue.

27 She looks diligently through the film,

   And understands the X's and O's.

28 The fans rise up and call her crazy;

   Her husband praises her saying:

29 "Many wives scream loudly,

   But you are heard above them all."

30 Quarterbacks may call the plays,

   But a wife who knows the game, she shall be praised.

31 Give her a winning season,

   And let her husband praise her on the post-game show.

PROVERBS 31:10

"An excellent wife, who can find her?
For her worth is far above jewels."

NO STANDS

The best advice I ever received was from our first head coach's wife, Chris Lane. My husband was still in college when he took a job coaching at a private school in our hometown where we met Coach Lane and Ms. Chris. They became very good friends of ours. She taught me many lessons; the first and most beneficial is "do not sit with the fans in the stands." She told me the story below.

"My husband was so excited about his first head coaching job, and I have to say I was excited about being a head coach's wife. He had taken over a team that was 1-19, 0-10 the year we took over. What were we thinking? As the season progressed, we won a couple of games and were feeling pretty good. I was sitting in the stands with a dear friend cheering and enjoying the game when our quarterback threw an interception. Suddenly over the loudspeaker, I heard these words: 'Run it. Run it. Run it. And now you throw it?' Everyone in the stadium heard these words including my husband. He promptly turned around and said to the announcer, 'You do the announcing, and I will do the coaching.' I slinked out of the stands and I *never* went back."

To be an "excellent coach's wife," we must separate ourselves from the noise. The fans always seem to know what play should have been called and who should be playing. Although they have been playing golf all week, working other jobs, and not watching film or practicing like the coaches have. Sitting in the stands only causes anxiety, tension, strife, and sometimes requires bail money. Some wives sit near the end zone or on the track or grass, and some do sit in the stands. Some schools have a reserved seating section that is just for coach's wives and families. This helps them to ignore the negative noise and embrace the positive cheering.

In our daily lives, we must remember to remove ourselves from the noise. We cannot see God or hear His play call with all the voices around us. John 17 reminds us that we are in the world but not of the world.

HOW DO YOU SEPARATE FROM THE WORLD WHILE STILL OPERATING IN IT?

_____

_____

_____

_____

_____

_____

_____

_____

PRAYER

LORD, HELP ME REMEMBER TO KEEP MY MIND FOCUSED ON YOU. WHEN ALL THE NOISE AND CHAOS SWIRLS AROUND ME, REMIND ME THAT YOUR WAY IS EXCELLENT. YOU HAVE CALLED ME TO BE EXCELLENT.

PROVERBS 31:11

"The heart of her husband trusts in her,
and he will have no lack of gain."

WHO'S GOT YOUR BACK?

We were playing one of our cross-county rivals for a pre-season game. I had prepared myself all week to be calm, cool, and collected at the game. I was not going to scream and yell like I tended to do most of the time. I was going to be composed and act like a coach's wife should.

Ha! Yeah, right! These are all great intentions until fans get started.

At the time, my husband was the Offensive Coordinator for our team, a team he coached to a state championship and semi-final playoff almost every single year. We were playing this game at the visiting stadium, so we did not have our normal reserved seats away from the know-it-all fans. I got there early and went all the way to the top to sit by myself. I spread several blankets out so people would know not to sit near me, or so I thought they would get the message. Well, a large, loud-mouthed man came and sat near me. Before the game even started, he was talking about our offense.

"They ain't no good." "I don't like the plays that OC calls." I was doing okay just trying to block it out and take deep breaths—until he called my husband by name.

He said out loud, "I cannot stand that man." Oh boy, that did it. I stood up, grabbed my large football bag, and spun around on him so fast that he almost fell off the top bleachers. I looked him in his eyes and elbowed him in his large belly and said, "That man is my husband, and he most certainly knows what he is doing, and I have heard enough from you. You can talk about the play call or even the coach, but do not call him by his name and act as if you know him personally when you do not!"

I stomped down the stands to where our head coach's wife was sitting, and she knew something was wrong. I was boiling over. Then our booster club president came over. Everyone knew I had lost it on that crazy man. My plan was not to tell my husband about this incident. But after the game, as soon as I walked on the field, he said, "What happened in the stands?" Someone had already told him all about it. Of course, over the years, the story has grown and is told every football season.

A more positive example of "having his back" comes from Donita Meadows, wife of Coach Dave Meadows from Texas whom I met at the Pro Bowl many years after this experience. She had tips to handle these situations much better than I did. She told me the story of being a young coach's wife:

"A fellow seasoned coach's wife advised me to 'turn off my ears at games.' Don't listen to what is being said at games, and if you do hear something, act like you did not hear it. That was great advice, which I have always tried to follow. I could tell early on that words could really hurt me and my family if I allowed them. I also

PROVERBS 31:11

knew that if I responded negatively, what people would remember is what I said and how I reacted. What someone had said about the coach or players would not have been remembered. And a wife's negative response in the stands could place the coach in a difficult position—to take up for his wife maybe against a parent or fan. He just does not need to know everything that goes on in the stands."

HAVE YOU HAD A SIMILAR EXPERIENCE?

All coach's wives must endure crazy comments, and our husbands do like to know we have their back and love them regardless of the play call. You can be a little less intense than me and much more like Donita in handling the situation, but always be sure everyone knows who you support.

_____

_____

_____

_____

_____

_____

_____

_____

_____

_____

_____

PROVERBS 31:11

PRAYER

LORD, GUIDE ME IN MY REACTIONS TO NEGATIVE PEOPLE. I WANT TO BE LIKE DONITA AND "TURN MY EARS OFF" TO THOSE AROUND ME ON FRIDAY NIGHTS.

PROVERBS 31:12

*"She does him good and not evil
all the days of her life."*

STATUE OF LIBERTY

I was watching a college game with my husband one Saturday. They ran this cool play where the quarterback hid the ball behind his back with the other hand in the air. I said, "Wow, what is that play called?" He told me they called it the Statue of Liberty. I loved the play. I constantly asked him to run that play on Friday nights. It became an inside joke for us. One Friday night, I was able to get the keys to the press box at the field where he called plays from. I taped a huge Statue of Liberty poster right in the center of his line of sight. He of course did not see it until the beginning of the game. He has yet to call that play after ten years. He called it an evil trick, but I meant it for good. He really did enjoy the prank and still tells everyone about it ten years later.

Showing an interest in what others are interested in makes them feel special and important. To do good and not evil to the people we love does not take grand gestures or expensive gifts.

PROVERBS 31:12

Showing we care with little things is what does us good for all the days of our lives.

WHAT ARE SOME GOOD THINGS YOU HAVE DONE AND CONTINUE TO DO FOR YOUR HUSBAND DURING THE SEASON THAT ARE MEMORABLE FOR YEARS TO COME?

_____

_____

_____

_____

_____

_____

_____

_____

_____

_____

_____

_____

_____

_____

_____

PRAYER

FATHER, GIVE ME YOUR EYES TO SEE THE NEEDS OF THOSE AROUND ME. SHOW ME HOW TO DO GOOD FOR THOSE I LOVE ON A DAILY BASIS.

PROVERBS 31:13

*"She looks for wool and linen
and works with her hands in delight."*

ROLL UP YOUR SLEEVES

One commentator states in relation to Proverbs 31:13 that a virtuous woman is not above dirtying her hands and working hard at manual labor. This woman does not need much done for her. She sees a need and rolls up her sleeves and attacks a project.[1]

This is true of all the coach's wives I know. God has given us the tools of strong personalities and streaks of extreme independence. Whether it is working the concession stand, washing smelly laundry, cleaning locker rooms, putting up bulletin boards, vacuuming nasty field houses, or driving hours to a game and home late at night in the dark all alone, we all say, "We got this." "Get out of my way and let me do this." Because our husbands are gone a large part of the time, we have learned to be very self-sufficient. We know how to do what we need or at least who to call to get the job done. Sometimes we can

---

1 "Proverbs 31:13," Let God Be True (website), accessed February 6, 2023, https://letgodbetrue.com/proverbs/index/chapter-31/proverbs-31-13/.

PROVERBS 31:13

become very frustrated with our situation because we feel alone or we feel as if we must "do it all."

But, according to the following verse, if God has called us to this role of coach's wife, He has equipped us to handle all that it entails with willing hands. 2 Corinthians 12:8-10 says, "My grace is sufficient for you, for my power is made perfect in weakness" (NIV).

WHAT HAVE YOU HAD TO ROLL UP YOUR SLEEVES AND TACKLE LATELY? HOW HAS GOD EQUIPPED YOU WITH THE TOOLS YOU NEED TO GET THE JOB DONE?

_____

_____

_____

_____

_____

_____

_____

_____

_____

_____

_____

_____

_____

PRAYER

THANK YOU, LORD, THAT YOUR STRENGTH IS PERFECT. I CALL ON YOU AND CLAIM THAT STRENGTH TODAY AS I WALK THROUGH THE FIRE.

PROVERBS 31:14

"She is like merchant ships;
she brings her food from afar."

DO YOU NEED APPLIANCES?

During our most recent move due to a job change, I was calling real estate agents in the local area to find a home to rent temporarily. This was a very small town. The real estate market was not on fire by any stretch of the imagination. After many calls with the same response of "Honey, we don't have much to rent here that you would want to live in" (with a strong Southern drawl), I finally got to my last straw.

One agent said, "Well, you know what, I may have something that would work. Do you need appliances though?" *What? You mean like a stove, a kitchen!? Well, yes, I think I will need that. Especially since there were only two restaurants in the nearby area. Are you kidding me?* I gave up at that point and just accepted that we would be living in a tent! I would truly be bringing my food from afar! After many calls and much searching, God provided a beautiful home for us. It even had a kitchen with appliances! Imagine my surprise!

PROVERBS 31:14

Jehovah-Jireh provides. Philippians 4:19 says, "And my God will supply all your needs according to His riches in glory in Christ Jesus."

All coach's wives have experienced something like this as moving often is part of the job. How we handle it is what counts.

ARE YOU ABLE TO LAUGH THROUGH IT AND KNOW GOD HAS IT COVERED?

That is what I have found helps me the most. A good laugh and a good cry, then I get up again and continue my "merchant ship" journey.

PRAYER

GOD, I WANT TO BE LIKE THE MERCHANT SHIP, CONTINUING MY JOURNEY EVEN WHEN THINGS ARE DIFFICULT, PUSHING THROUGH THE MURKY WATERS TO BRING MY FAMILY WHAT THEY NEED, AND DEPENDING ON JEHOVAH-JIREH EVERY STEP OF THE WAY.

PROVERBS 31:15

"And she rises while it is still night and gives food to her household, and portions to her attendants."

WHAT SLEEP?

After home games on Friday nights, we always gather as football staff and families to eat a very late dinner. When this tradition started many years ago, we would all go back to the head coach's house. We soon outgrew that and began using the cafeteria at the school. When we moved away for a short period, we started this tradition at our new school, and everyone came to my house after the games on Friday nights. Now we are back home and once again using the cafeteria after the games.

This is a great tradition that allows everyone to decompress after a stressful week and stressful game. We have seen God use this time to bring us closer during losses and hard times and allow us to celebrate together during wins and good times. All the families love it and always ask, "What's on the menu?" They always make requests for their favorite foods.

While this is a lot of fun and an integral part of our football family tradition, it is also a lot of work on those of us who host and prepare.

I have stayed up late into the night or risen extra early in the morning to prepare "food for my football household and portions for the coaches." I do enjoy picking the themes and making menus each week. All the wives contribute a dish based on our theme, and some have a must-have dish that must be present every week. For us, the two must-haves are ice-cream cake and cheese dip.

This time together fosters friendships and creates relationship bonds between all our families. We hope to continue this tradition for as long as we are coaching.

WHAT TRADITIONS ARE YOU PART OF THAT MAY REQUIRE YOU TO "RISE WHILE IT IS STILL NIGHT"? HOW ARE YOU SEEING GOD WORK THROUGH THESE TIMES?

_____
_____
_____
_____
_____
_____
_____
_____
_____
_____
_____

PRAYER

FATHER, GIVE ME THE ENERGY TO CONTINUE TO RISE EARLY AND STAY UP LATE. I WANT TO SERVE MY HOUSEHOLD OF COACHES AND FAMILIES WELL.

PROVERBS 31:16

"She considers a field and buys it;
from her earnings she plants a vineyard."

BLOOM WHERE YOU ARE PLANTED

In this day and time, most of us do not "consider fields" for purchase. But we do consider homes. In our lives in the coaching world, we move a lot. In my experience, most every move, I have been the one to "consider the house and buy it." He has always already been at the new school and is deep in getting all the football stuff ready, so house-buying and "considering" falls to me. It does help that I am a licensed Realtor. Generally, I say, "Here is the new address, see you there." I have had to sign as power of attorney on many occasions because closing occurred during spring practice. I am thankful God gives me wisdom and confidence in the process of finding a home for our family.

Donita Meadows, wife of Coach Dave Meadows, has experienced moving more times than most of us. In the span of ten years, they were members at three different churches in three different cities. Upon arrival at each of these churches, God gave them Jeremiah 29:11 to hold onto: "'For I know the plans I have for you,' declares

PROVERBS 31:16

the Lord, 'plans to prosper you and not to harm you, plans to give you hope and a future.'" During this same time, a new friend arrived at her door with a plant and package of seeds with a card that said, "Bloom where you are planted." God reminded her through this that He places us by divine intervention. We are to consider the places He has put us and bloom there for His glory.

HOW IS GOD HELPING YOU TO BLOOM WHERE HE HAS PLANTED YOU FOR THIS SEASON?

_____
_____
_____
_____
_____
_____
_____
_____
_____
_____
_____
_____
_____

PRAYER

THANK YOU, GOD, FOR GIVING ME THE CONFIDENCE AND PERMISSION IN THIS VERSE TO CONSIDER WHAT IS BEST FOR MY FAMILY AND TO DO IT WITH BOLDNESS AND FAITH IN MY ABILITY THROUGH YOU TO MAKE WISE DECISIONS. I WANT TO BLOOM WHERE YOU PLANT ME.

PROVERBS 31:17

"She surrounds her waist with strength
and makes her arms strong."

STRONG ARMS

Patsy Nix, wife of Coach Conrad Nix, tells of a time she was thankful for physical strength and strong arms.

"It has always been a tradition to join my husband on the field after the game to congratulate or console him. At one game, I went to the gate leading to the field and told the nice police officer that I was Coach Nix's wife, and I always met my husband on the field. He told me I could not go on the field. No one was allowed on the field. However, everyone on the opposing side was going on the field. He told me he was not allowed to let us onto the field. He locked the gate and walked away.

"There was a brick wall around the stands. I took my niece, put her on the ledge, and lowered her to the field below with my 'strong arms.' I sat on the ledge and jumped down to the field. My ten-year-old niece, Amber, was so excited for the adventure, but I was just a determined coach's wife trying to get to my husband on the field. On the way home, Amber told her dad that Aunt Patsy was going to jail because the police officer said we could not go on the field. I had a hard time explaining that one. Including this game, I have never missed a game getting on the field to give my husband a hug and kiss in victory or defeat."

As coach's wives, it is important that we are physically strong because our husbands are away from home so often, many duties that require physical strength fall to us. Getting down Christmas decorations, putting up the tree, packing moving boxes, unpacking moving boxes, carrying sleeping children from the car after a long game, and yes, even climbing a fence to get on the field. All these are realities in our world, and we need strength to get them done.

CAN YOU THINK OF OTHER THINGS IN YOUR COACHING-WIFE LIFE THAT HAVE REQUIRED PHYSICAL STRENGTH? WHAT ARE YOU DOING TO "GIRD YOURSELF WITH STRENGTH AND MAKE YOUR ARMS STRONG"?

_____

_____

_____

_____

_____

_____

_____

_____

_____

PRAYER

THANK YOU, LORD, FOR PHYSICAL STRENGTH. THANK YOU FOR GIVING ME WHAT I NEED TO GET THINGS DONE ON MY OWN WHEN NEEDED. YOU ARE MY STRENGTH AND MY PORTION. I CRY OUT TO YOU AND ASK YOU TO STRENGTHEN ME SPIRITUALLY AND PHYSICALLY DAILY.

PROVERBS 31:18

"She senses that her profit is good;
her lamp does not go out at night."

SLEEP/REST

"Her lamp does not go out at night." *What? Does this lady not sleep?* It certainly sounds like it, but no way could it be. We must sleep and rest to function properly. I need six to eight hours of sleep at night, or I am a very cranky person. I am an early-to-bed, early-to-rise type of girl. Usually in bed by nine p.m. and up by five a.m.

I *do* "turn my lamp off" at night. The Proverbs 31 woman is not idle even when night falls. She is working day and night, as we like to say. I know many times I feel as though I am working 24/7! With my paying jobs and the other full-time job as a coach's wife, it feels never-ending.

Yes, God expects us to work and not be idle. He gives us creative minds and gifts and talents to use for His glory. But I also know He calls us to rest. Physical rest as well as spiritual rest is vital to properly do the jobs He has called us to do.

PROVERBS 31:18

ARE YOU TIRED? ARE YOU WEARY? IS IT MID-SEASON AND YOU FEEL LIKE IT IS NEVER GOING TO END? IS YOUR LAMP LITERALLY NOT GOING OUT AT NIGHT?

Take time to sleep and rest in Christ. He will renew and restore you. He says, "Come to me and I will give you rest."

_____

_____

_____

_____

_____

_____

_____

_____

_____

_____

_____

_____

_____

_____

_____

_____

PRAYER

FATHER, THANK YOU FOR RENEWING AND RESTORING ME.

PROVERBS 31:19

"She stretches out her hand to the distaff,
and her hands grasp the spindle."

WORKER BEE

This woman was a worker bee. This verse is a picture of her spinning yarn to make garments. Most of us probably do not spin yarn in the literal sense, but we do the physical work that it takes to take care of our household. Maybe you are a stay-at-home mom taking care of your children all day. Maybe you are a schoolteacher working with students all day. Maybe you are a businesswoman working deals. Whatever profession you have, you are also a coach's wife, which in and of itself is a full-time job. Sometimes it feels like there are not enough hours in the day to get all the jobs done. We are just trying to keep our heads above water. Many times, I have felt like this. God has been teaching me to wait on Him and He will work it all out. I am not a model student. I am a "worker bee" at heart. I feel that if I am still and waiting, I am missing something, or I should be doing something. God constantly reminds me of Psalm 46:10, "Be still, and know that I am God" (ESV).

PROVERBS 31:19

DO YOU FEEL THIS WAY? ARE YOU A WORKER BEE OR ARE YOU ABLE TO SIT AND WAIT ON THE FATHER? HOW MIGHT YOU STRIVE FOR A BALANCE BETWEEN THE TWO?

_____

_____

_____

_____

_____

_____

_____

_____

_____

_____

_____

_____

_____

_____

_____

_____

_____

PRAYER

FATHER, HELP ME TO REMEMBER THAT IN MY WORKING, THERE IS ALSO WAITING. I WANT TO WAIT ON YOU AND YOUR DIRECTION SO ALL MY WORK IS NOT IN VAIN.

PROVERBS 31:20

"She extends her hand to the poor,
and she stretches out her hands to the needy."

WHERE ARE YOU CALLED TO SERVE?

As coach's wives, we are in servants' roles whether we choose to be or not. There are many things we do out of necessity and not because of a calling or true willingness. We help in the concession stand, we set up for tailgates, we cook for after-game parties, we entertain other wives and families on game day, we take care of each other's children, etc. Which are all great things, and much needed in the extended coach's family. Most coach's wives generally have a servant's heart, and they give the gift of hospitality as Peter directs in 1 Peter 4:9 to "be hospitable to one another without complaint" (ESV). But what do you have outside of the coaching world?

For me, it is Ronald McDonald House Charities. I was first made aware of this organization when one of our very good friends and fellow coaching family had a sick child. We visited them at a Ronald McDonald House. I was really impressed with the organization. A few months after this visit, it was New Year's Day in church and our pastor asked the question, "What will you do this year totally for someone else that has nothing to do with your immediate daily life?" Ronald McDonald House came to mind. I contacted our local chapter and began volunteering twice per month from six to nine p.m. on Wednesday nights. In eight years, I have very seldom missed a night. This is something totally away from football or my coach's-wife life that allows me an outlet to help others and serve as God calls us to do.

WHAT IS YOUR SERVANT OUTLET OR CALLING OUTSIDE OF YOUR COACHING-WIFE BUBBLE?

If you do not have one, pray about how and where God would have you serve.

_____

_____

_____

_____

_____

_____

_____

_____

_____

_____

_____

_____

PRAYER

FATHER, I WANT TO BE YOUR HANDS AND FEET AND SERVE THOSE YOU PUT IN MY PATH. TEACH ME TO GIVE HOSPITALITY WITHOUT COMPLAINT.

PROVERBS 31:21

"She is not afraid of the snow for her household,
for all her household are clothed with scarlet."

NO RED

"Clothed in scarlet" refers to the wool used by Moses in the Old Testament. It is also said to represent the blood Jesus shed to cleanse us of our sins. It was a rare color of its time and indicated luxury and wealth. Colors held great meaning in biblical times, almost as much meaning as school colors hold to us as coaching families.

Our current team colors are navy, orange, and white. Most every school we have been part of except for one has been primarily blue. The two schools where my husband has been the head coach have had big rival schools whose primary color is red. So for over twenty years, I have not been able to wear red of any kind. I love red in clothing and shoes, but I have very little of it in my closet. I will wear a red sweater at Christmas time if we will not be near the school. "Thou shall not wear red" is a school moto, and they are not kidding. It is serious business. If you are wearing red, it means you are rooting for the other team, and you should move to that side of town. Maybe one day we will get to wear red again. Who knows?

Clothing our families physically to be prepared for the right type of weather is very important. However, clothing them spiritually is life changing. The Proverbs 31 woman worked to prepare her family for the spiritual winters of life, the hardships and trials she knew would come. She had no fear of the literal cold or the spiritual cold because she was teaching her family how to lean on the Lord and His Word in all situations.

HOW ARE YOU CLOTHING YOURSELF AND YOUR FAMILY WITH ALL THAT IS NEEDED PHYSICALLY, SPIRITUALLY, AND EMOTIONALLY TO BE PREPARED FOR EVERY SEASON? NO MATTER THE COLOR OF THE CLOTHING, IS IT FIT FOR THE SEASON?

_____
_____
_____
_____
_____
_____
_____
_____
_____
_____
_____
_____

PRAYER

FATHER, I PRAY THAT MY FAMILY IS CLOTHED IN YOUR BLOOD. I PRAY THAT THEY FEEL LUXURIOUS AND WEALTHY IN YOUR SIGHT. I PRAY THAT THEY HAVE NO FEAR OF THE SEASON BECAUSE THEY ARE CLINGING TO YOUR WORD.

PROVERBS 31:22

"She makes coverings for herself;
her clothing is fine linen and purple."

LOOK GOOD, FEEL GOOD, PLAY GOOD

My brother was a star high school football player. He went on to play for the University of Georgia and was later drafted into the NFL. He is now the head coach of his high school alma mater. Through his entire career from midget league football all the way to the NFL, his mantra was "look good, feel good, play good." He wanted the best gear, matching wrist bands, and all the other must-have items. My mom made sure he had what he needed to "look good, feel good, and play good." We often tease each other about this phrase on and off the field.

This is, however, a great image for our lives as coach's wives. There have been many times when I just don't feel like it. I don't want to go the game and smile and act happy and cheer again. I don't want to have dinner with the other coaches' families tonight. I am feeling old, worn, and tired. All valid feelings that, if you are in the game long enough, you are sure to experience. But we must put on our "fine linen and purple" and look good, feel good, play good one more time.

Kim Moore, wife of Coach Greg Moore, states that when things don't turn out like we hoped, our purpose still remains. Our story is not over. We must stay in the story where God has placed us.

Your presence is an encouragement to those around you. It is not the place but the people that make our lives so rich. The lives we impact inspire us to keep going.

Next time you feel like you just can't make it through another game or another season, go to your mirror and put on your best game clothes and favorite lipstick and say to yourself, "Look good, feel good, play good."

DURING THESE TIMES OF DOUBT AND DISCOURAGEMENT AS THE SEASON GROWS LONG, HOW CAN YOU STAY IN THE STORY?

_____

_____

_____

_____

_____

_____

_____

_____

_____

_____

PRAYER

FATHER, AS THE SEASON GROWS LONG, I NEED YOUR HELP TO STAY IN THE STORY. GIVE ME WHAT I NEED TO HAVE THE ENERGY AND DESIRE TO LOOK GOOD, FEEL GOOD, PLAY GOOD JUST ONE MORE NIGHT.

PROVERBS 31:23

"Her husband is known in the gates,
when he sits among the elders of the land."

DO YOU IRON?

"I DO NOT IRON!" I told my husband when we were dating. "I do not know how."

He asked me to iron a dress shirt for him before going to church one afternoon. First and last time he asked that. He wanted creases down the arms. Well, he got creases and wrinkles everywhere. I put more wrinkles in it than I took out! You may think I did this on purpose just so he would never ask again, but no, I was not that smart. I just DO NOT IRON. This can be a dilemma in my marriage because my husband is very particular about his clothing. Especially his Friday-night game clothes. So, many years ago, we decided it best for all involved to allow the professionals to handle his game clothes. For the last twenty years, I have taken his game pants and game shirt to the dry cleaners every Monday morning and picked them up every Thursday morning. I hang them in his closet nicely pressed with creases down the legs for Friday night.

Now, I many not actually do the ironing myself, but I make sure he looks good in "his gate" on Friday nights.

There are many behind-the-scenes activities coach's wives take care of that allow our husbands to "be known in the gates." Maybe you work a full-time job to supplement income while taking care of the children. Maybe you work the gates or concession stands at games. Maybe you help with fundraising. Maybe you keep the stats or the books. Whatever your role is, God is using you to impact the lives of others in His gates.

WHAT ROLE HAS GOD PLACED YOU IN THIS SEASON TO BRING GLORY IN HIS GATES?

Ask Him to show you clearly how to honor Him in the role you have been given.

_____
_____
_____
_____
_____
_____
_____
_____
_____
_____

PRAYER

FATHER, USE ME IN ANY WAY YOU SEE FIT. I DO NOT NEED TO BE SEEN TO KNOW THAT MY WORK IS IMPACTING LIVES. HELP ME TO FEEL CONFIDENT IN KNOWING THAT THE ROLE YOU GIVE TO ME IS THE MOST IMPORTANT AT THE TIME FOR YOUR GLORY.

PROVERBS 31:24

"She makes linen garments and sells them, and supplies belts to the tradesmen."

JEHOVAH-JIREH

Have you been in the coaching life long enough to have gotten the dreaded call? The one that punches you in the gut and literally takes your breath away: "Honey, I was fired..."

If you have, you know how horrible those words are to hear, but you also know that eventually there is joy on the other side. Are you prepared with "garments to sell and items to provide to the tradesmen" to keep your family afloat for a while? Has God gifted you with a talent or job that allows you to provide for your family when the rug is pulled out from under you in this coaching world? Being fired has many repercussions for the family, but one of the main fears is financial. *How will we pay our bills? What about insurance?* All valid fears and normal thoughts. Even in the face of these fears, we know God is Jehovah-Jireh. He will provide.

During our most recent "transition," my husband was three months without a paycheck. Yes, three months! That is a long time. I was just getting back into my real estate career after a two-year break because of a previous move. Before we even packed the moving trucks to head to our new location, God sent me two clients. By the time the three months were up without my husband's paycheck, God had blessed me with more closings than I had ever had in my fifteen years as a Realtor. Despite our worry and concern, God showed Himself as Jehovah-Jireh big time.

WHEN HAS GOD PROVIDED FOR YOU BY PREPARING YOU WITH A JOB OR TALENT OR SAVINGS?

Thank Him for His provision and timing.

_____

_____

_____

_____

_____

_____

_____

_____

_____

_____

_____

PRAYER

GOD, THANK YOU FOR ALWAYS PROVIDING FOR OUR NEEDS. EVEN BEFORE WE KNOW WE NEED IT, YOU ARE ALREADY THERE.

PROVERBS 31:25

"Strength and dignity are her clothing,
and she smiles at the future."

CIRCLE UP

I read the book *The Circle Maker* by Mark Batterson about a year ago. The concept is based on Joshua marching around the walls of Jericho seven times until the walls fell. The author tells of times in his life when he has devoted total prayer to an issue and "circled it up." After reading this book, I created a circle board and put some specific things I was praying for on the board. The biggest and main prayer in the center, and others on the outside.

For over a year, I had the letter N in the middle of the circle, symbolizing my husband's dream job. We had been praying for this opportunity for many years before I knew about the circle concept. But the circle board symbolized praying circles around his heart's desire.

A few months prior to him getting the job, God spoke clearly to me and said, "Walk the circle." I went one to two times per week to the campus and walked around the school seven times. I had seven individual index cards with Scriptures I prayed for each circle. I was

PROVERBS 31:25

trying to walk with "strength and dignity and smile at the future." Some days this was easier than others. Many days there were tears shed on each circle around. It seemed like we would never see this prayer answered. Finally, God answered, and we got the job. God was faithful, and as a good friend points out, "God rewards obedience."

WHAT IS THERE THAT YOU NEED TO "CIRCLE UP"? HOW CAN YOU DISPLAY STRENGTH AND DIGNITY AND SMILE AT THE FUTURE?

_____

_____

_____

_____

_____

_____

_____

_____

_____

_____

_____

_____

PRAYER

GOD, THANK YOU THAT YOU HONOR BOLD PRAYERS AND OBEDIENCE. THANK YOU THAT WE CAN SMILE AT THE FUTURE EVEN WHEN WE DO NOT KNOW WHAT IT HOLDS.

PROVERBS 31:26

"She opens her mouth in wisdom,
and the teaching of kindness is on her tongue."

CAROLYN CURRY KIND OF KIND

I don't know about you, but for me, this type of kindness and wisdom talked about in Proverbs 31 is not in my nature. I have a very hard time being kind when people are being unkind to me and especially to my husband. As a coach's family, we have all been there. Fans can be brutal. I tend to become very defensive, and generally when I open my mouth, the words that come out would not be considered "wise or kind" by the Prov. 31 standard.

We recently had the opportunity to join one of our boosters in his box at a GA Tech game. Also there that day was Coach Bill Curry and his wife Dr. Carolyn Curry. Coach Curry played at Georgia Tech and in the NFL. Later he became the head coach for Georgia Tech, Alabama, Kentucky, and Georgia State University. Dr. Carolyn Curry is an award-winning author and nonprofit founder. We were talking about how difficult it is for wives and families to be in the stands with all the harsh words and crazy comments from fans. Carolyn said she always liked to sit in the stands to be close to the action, but Coach Curry said he finally had to insist that she move to the boxes in Alabama because he was afraid she would get hurt. You see, she has a very sweet, genuine nature. She had a gift for dealing with those fans talking about her husband. At the beginning of the game, when she could identify *the one* who was the loudest and foulest, she would walk right over and sit next to them, put her hand on their shoulder and say in her sweet but firm southern drawl, "Hi, I am Carolyn Curry. That is my husband out there. Now, we are not going to have any of this kind of talk today, do you understand?" Often, she got a confused and stunned "yes, ma'am" in return. Now that is the wisdom and kindness of Prov. 31.

I have not actually tried this yet, but maybe this season I will.

HOW CAN YOU USE THIS METHOD OR A VARIATION OF IT TO DIFFUSE STRIFE THIS SEASON?

If you use the "Carolyn Curry" method of kindness, please share your results with all of us striving to "open our mouths in wisdom and kindness."

_____

_____

_____

_____

_____

_____

_____

PRAYER

FATHER, THIS IS SO DIFFICULT FOR ME. PLEASE HELP ME TO HAVE THE TEACHING OF WISDOM AND KINDNESS ON MY TONGUE. REMIND ME TO KEEP MY MOUTH CLOSED MOST OF THE TIME.

PROVERBS 31:27

"She watches over the activities of her household, and does not eat the bread of idleness."

CHEESE SANDWICH

It finally happened! We got the dream job. The one we prayed "circles" around. My husband has wanted to be head coach at this school for more than ten years. He began his career here and then left for other jobs along our coaching journey. But God gave him a desire in his heart to come back here. We prayed and we hoped for so many years and were let down several times. But, finally in God's timing, it happened this week. We knew it was going to be confirmed on Tuesday afternoon at Board of Education meeting. So, you would think the coach's wife would have a great celebratory dinner planned. Well, not this time. I teach fitness and yoga classes at night. Tuesday night is my yoga class. I went to yoga class as normal after seeing him at school for a quick congratulations. I did decorate his home office for a surprise when he got home, but no big party or special dinner this night. He came home to an empty house and made himself a cheese sandwich. When written this way, it sounds very sad, and I seem to be an awful wife. But we laugh at it. When people asked,

"Did y'all have a big dinner?" or "What did y'all do?" he says very dramatically, "I had a cheese sandwich."

This job was and is a big deal for our family, and we are very excited and grateful. However, our lives do not stop or alter on a weeknight. We have a party and dinner planned soon.

I do strive to watch over the activities of my household and not "eat the bread of idleness." It says nothing about cheese and bread.

HOW DO YOU WATCH OVER THE ACTIVITIES OF YOUR HOUSEHOLD AND TAKE CARE OF YOURSELF IN OUR CRAZY COACHING WORLD?

___

___

___

___

___

___

___

___

___

___

___

___

PRAYER

FATHER, HELP ME TO ALWAYS
LOOK WELL TO THE WAYS OF MY
HOUSEHOLD. SHOW ME YOUR WAYS.

PROVERBS 31:28

"Her children rise up and bless her."

HAND ON YOUR HEART AND DUMB PLAYS

"Hand on your heart, hand on your heart," my three-year-old nephew commands as he stands in the loft area of our mountain cabin with a humongous pair of white boxer shorts attached to a long pole. Sixteen-plus adults below comply with the order as we all sing "The Star-Spangled Banner."

This funny scene occurred during Christmas vacation with our entire family a few years ago. His daddy is a football coach, and at every game during the national anthem, his grandmother has always told him, "Put your hand on your heart." He does not know many nursery rhymes or kid songs, but he knows "The Star-Spangled Banner" because he has heard it every fall Friday night of his life.

Chris Lane, wife of Coach Bruce Lane, tells a story about her son, Christian. "When he was younger, Christian always had his own football game going on during his dad's game. At different times during the game, he would run over to me and ask, 'Mom, who is winning?' 'What is the score?' Then he would run back to his game. One night, when he was eight years old, I looked up to see him running off the sidelines. I ran over to ask him what he was doing on the field. He said, 'I was just asking Dad who keeps calling those dumb plays!'"

Coach's kids live very different lives from most of their friends. Most who I know love it and dive in to all it has to offer. They love to be on the field with Dad on Friday nights. They also come to understand over time that Mom is the one holding it all together. Pretty much by herself, most of the time. Mom is the one who carries the weight of day-to-day activities and makes sure all is in order while Dad is immersed in coaching. While the children are young, they may not realize or notice. But as they grow older and wiser, they see the work and support for the entire family, and they will literally rise up and bless her.

If you are feeling discouraged today with all of the responsibility, remember that one day your children will rise up and bless you!

HOW HAVE YOUR CHILDREN ALREADY RISEN UP TO BLESS YOU?

_____

_____

_____

_____

_____

_____

_____

_____

PRAYER

FATHER, HELP ME TO MOLD MY
CHILDREN IN YOUR IMAGE.
GIVE ME THE VISION I NEED TO SEE
THAT ONE DAY ALL OF THE WORK
WILL BE REWARDED.

PROVERBS 31:29

*"Many daughters have done nobly,
but you excel them all."*

ROLE MODELS

In the past twenty-two years of coaching, we have marched with the Trojans, soared with the Eagles, warred with the Warriors, prowled with the Panthers, fought with the Vikings, roared with the Tigers, and are presently once again soaring with the Eagles.

Through all the mascot changes, our hearts have remained unchanged. We love the school we are a part of in any given season. We love the players as our own children. We mentor the coaches and their wives. We dive into the community headfirst. All the schools hold special places in our hearts and memories in our minds. There are those, of course, that hold fonder memories than others.

There are football wives who have taught me over the years how to love and support my husband and how not to lose my mind in this crazy life some people call a game.

Chris Lane was my first teacher. She taught me that nowhere is too far. Pack up the car and drive to the game alone with your young child if you must. But the drive is even better with family or friends or another coach's wife. The game being "too far" or "in the middle of nowhere" is no excuse. She also taught me the most valuable lesson of being a coach's wife: "DO NOT SIT WITH THE FANS!"

Patsy Nix is definitely the First Lady of high school football in Georgia. She has been in the trenches for many years. She took me under her wing in the early years when I was in a new town and did not know a soul. She taught me the importance of hospitality and how to feed everyone after Friday-night games. I watched her show unconditional love to her husband and family. Through all the wins and even during our few losses, she always walked with her head held high and had quiet encouragement for all the coaches and wives.

Kim Moore is the sweetest head coach's wife I know. I had the privilege of learning from her for only one season, but in that short time, her influence had a great impact. Kim hosted coaches and wives and their children in her home and made everyone feel like family. She made being a mother to young children, working a full-time job, and being the head coach's wife look like a breeze. She did it all with grace and beauty.

Laurie Kinsler has always kept me laughing. She is passionate and vocal when it comes to supporting her husband. She taught me to be fierce and "always have my husband's back," even when we may not agree. I learned lessons from Laurie on long, late-night trips from games. I saw her be an honest critic in private but always a vocal supporter in public.

I have called on these ladies many times during our career. They continue to be a source of support, advice, and friendship.

PROVERBS 31:29

I covet their prayers for me as I also lift them up during our busy season of life.

My goal is to pass on the lessons I have learned from Chris, Patsy, Kim, and Laurie to those who I currently serve. I want to show the same support, encouragement, and love that was shown to me for so many years.

WHO ARE YOU THANKFUL TO GOD FOR AS A ROLE MODEL IN YOUR COACH'S-WIFE LIFE?

_____
_____
_____
_____
_____
_____
_____
_____
_____
_____
_____
_____
_____

PROVERBS 31:29

PRAYER

FATHER, THANK YOU FOR THOSE WHO HAVE WALKED BEFORE US. THANK YOU FOR THEIR EXAMPLE AND THEIR PERSEVERANCE.

PROVERBS 31:30

"Charm is deceitful and beauty is vain, but a woman who fears the Lord, she shall be praised."

"PRETTY IS AS PRETTY DOES"

"Pretty is as pretty does" are the words of my mother throughout my entire childhood and into adulthood. In the coaching world, sometimes it seems that charm and charisma are half the battle when it comes to getting jobs. Our husbands must show charm and charisma, and we as wives are expected to be charming and beautiful standing beside him. Even in the worst seasons, where we lose every game and fans are screaming for our heads on a platter, we are still expected to smile and bear the pressure with grace and beauty. However, what we show on the outside is not always what we are feeling on the inside. We generally hide our true feelings very well due to years of practice.

Charm and beauty may get the job in the beginning, but they do not go very far in helping to keep the job. The new wears off quickly, and soon people can see underneath. My face generally shows my exact thoughts and feelings. It is helpful for me to remember to Philippians 4:8 it. "Whatever is true, whatever is honorable, whatever is right, whatever is pure, whatever is lovely, whatever is commendable, if there is any excellence and if anything worthy of praise, think about these things."

Through good seasons and bad seasons, we must remember that fear of the Lord is most important. Praise does not come from charm or beauty in the eyes of God. We are to be praised when we fear, revere, and live for Him.

WHAT PHRASE OR MEMORY DO YOU HAVE THAT PUTS YOU IN YOUR PLACE WHEN YOU MAY LEAN TOWARD TRUSTING CHARM AND BEAUTY INSTEAD OF THE LORD?

_____

_____

_____

_____

_____

_____

_____

_____

_____

_____

_____

PRAYER

FATHER, I WANT TO BE A WOMAN WHO FEARS YOU. I WANT TO SHOW YOUR BEAUTY AND YOUR GLORY.

PROVERBS 31:31

"Give her the product of her hands,
and let her works praise her in the gates."

YOU **ARE** WELCOME

It has been said that behind every great coach is an even greater coach's wife. As coaches, our husbands have very public roles. They are known everywhere they go. People wait to hear them speak and want their opinion on everything. As wives, we are generally support staff. All the things we do to keep life running smoothly most of the time go unnoticed, and often, we may feel we are unappreciated.

The public wants to know who the quarterback is this year. What play will we run to beat our rival? Will we win it all this year? But they never ask,

- Who is packing lunches, getting kids up and ready, and taking them to school?
- Who is mowing the grass?
- Who is cooking dinner?
- Who is coaching the coach's nine-year-old son's team?

- Who is handling car maintenance and home maintenance appointments?
- Who is going to the grocery store?
- Who is feeding the family and the coaching staff and the team?
- Who is taking the forgotten shoes or clothes to the school for the tenth time this week?
- Who is taking care of extended family and attending family events alone?
- Who is attending the parent-teacher conference with the coach's kid?
- Who is making sure Friday-night coaching clothes are laundered each week?

We know who the *who* is. It is you; it is me; it is us, the coach's wives. If we don't do it, it does not get done. God has given the coach's wife a special heart and a grit to bear the burdens well. Sometimes I believe we might have a little crazy in us too to accept this insane life we live. All these things outside of the limelight are crucial for coaches, teams, and families of coaches to be successful.

Even though these may seem like thankless, meaningless tasks, they are some of the most important. For without success in the small everyday matters, there could not be the Friday-night successes. So, on your next Friday-night win, know you were a big part and "let your works praise you in the gates" of the field.

After your next win, just go right up to your husband with a big smile and say, "YOU ARE WELCOME!"

PRAYER

FATHER, REMIND ME THAT ALL THAT I DO IS FOR YOUR GLORY. IT IS NOT ABOUT ME OR FOR ME. IT IS ALL FOR YOU.

ACKNOWLEDGMENTS

Walking with You Through Every Season took me five years to complete. God prompted me to write this book three coaching jobs ago. Looking at the size of it makes one wonder why it took so long. A large part of the reason is my procrastination and thoughts of *Is it good enough for others to want to read? Is this really relevant to others?* This process also took a while because within the last five years my husband has changed coaching jobs three times and we have moved two times. We have had other trials that set my timeline back like family illnesses for extended periods of time, COVID-19, and other general interruptions and distractions of daily life. All of these trials have helped to add to the stories and lessons of the book.

I am deeply indebted to my friend and fellow author Chrissie Tomlinson. Chrissie encouraged me to keep writing even when I did not feel like anyone would want to read this. She helped me take all the random words on the page and organize them to make sense. In her wisdom she would say, "Hurry up and finish, there's someone out there who needs this book." Chrissie was my first editor and

ACKNOWLEDGMENTS

guide through the writing process. She is a seasoned author and gave up a lot of her time to help this newbie. Chrissie was, and is my teacher, guide, prayer warrior, and encourager. Without her, this book would not exist.

A huge thank-you to Abigail Thompson. Abigail is an extraordinary young lady and fellow author. Abigail did hours of research to get her own book published. She gave of her time and resources to point me in the direction of professional editors, formatters, and publishers. Abigail helped to simplify the process for me when I was totally overwhelmed. Her knowledge and expertise of the business has been invaluable to me.

Jana Shugart is one of my most favorite people on the planet. I have known her all my life. I have watched her grow from a little girl into an amazing woman of God. She was an encourager to me through this writing process. She read several drafts and gave me some great feedback. She shared her path as an author and helped guide me to listen to what God was telling me to write.

To all the coaches' wives who contributed stories and anecdotes and gave me permission to use their stories, this book is for you. Chris Lane, Patsy Nix, Donita Meadows, Kim Moore, and Carolyn Curry I am so thankful God placed you in my life at the perfect time and saw fit to use you to teach me so much about Himself. We have a unique perspective and a unique set of needs because of this job and ministry God has called our families to. Thank you for sharing your hearts with me and allowing me to use small parts of your lives in this book. Thank you to those of you who took the time to read

ACKNOWLEDGMENTS

through several drafts and help me to make needed changes to reflect the craziness of our lives and God's provision through it.

Finally, to my husband and best friend and biggest fan, Coach Chad Alligood. Chad is always encouraging me to write and to share what I have written. He loves sharing my blog and other writings with all his coaching connections. He believes everything I write will be at the top of the Amazon Best Seller list. He is my prayer warrior and encourager through every step of life.

God has truly done more than I could ever ask or imagine through this coaching life. I am forever thankful that He has placed amazing people in my life to encourage me to share what He has done.

ABOUT THE AUTHOR

Talisha Alligood currently resides in Centerville, GA, with her husband, Coach Chad Alligood. Many of the coaches' wives she has met over the twenty-five years and nine moves have contributed to *Walking with You Through Every Season* with stories and advice. In addition to the full-time job of being a coach's wife, Talisha is a licensed Realtor in the state of Georgia and holds a BS in Exercise Science and Physiology. Talisha is a trained Precept Upon Precept Inductive Bible Study leader and currently leads classes at First Baptist Church Centerville, GA. She has been a Bible Study leader and teacher for twenty years. Talisha is the founder of REST WELLNESS Retreats. She, along with her team, uses fitness and wellness to share God's love and the benefits of His rest with women across the country and Canada. Read more on her blog at https://proverbs31coacheswife.wordpress.com for posts associated with this devotional and encouragement for the coach's wife's life. Like and follow *Proverbs 31 Coach's Wife* on Facebook (Proverbs 31 Coach's Wife) and Instagram (@coachs_wife_ga.)

Made in the USA
Columbia, SC
22 February 2025